This book belongs to
_____

This book is dedicated to my children - Mikey, Kobe, and Jojo.

Copyright © 2024 by Grow Grit Press LLC. All rights reserved. No part of this book may be reproduced in any form without permission in writing from the publisher. Please send bulk order requests to growgritpress@gmail.com Printed and bound in the USA. MiniMovers.tv
Paperback ISBN: 978-1-63731-881-2 Hardcover ISBN: 978-1-63731-883-6

Maya Angelou

By Mary Nhin

Hi, I'm Maya Angelou.

I had a tough start in life, facing challenges that made me feel sad. But guess what?

I didn't let those challenges define me. I found something magical that helped me through it all - the power of words!

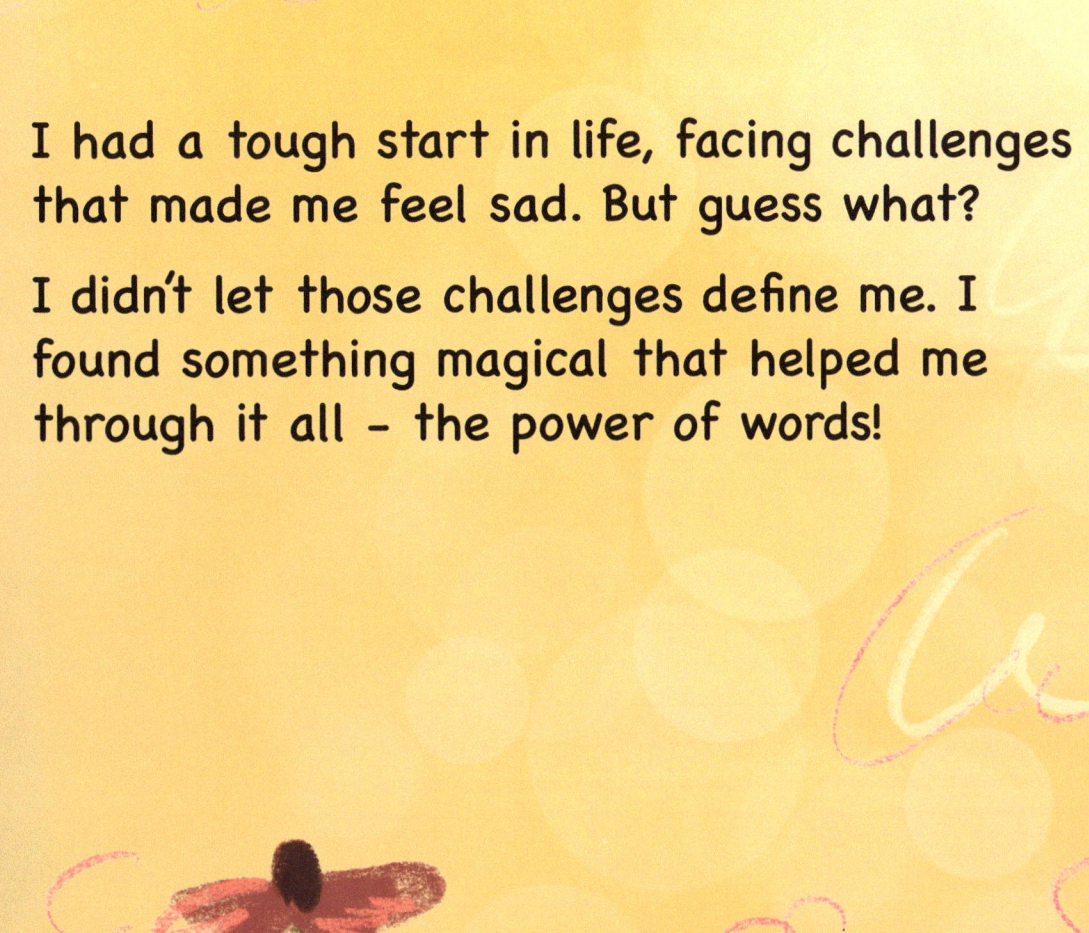

I fell in love with reading and writing. Words became my best friends, and I learned that they had the power to lift my spirit and make me feel strong.

My grandmother, who was my guiding star, told me...

Growing up, I faced some tough times, but I never gave up. I traveled the world, met amazing people, and learned many things. Every experience shaped the person I was becoming.

My love for words helped me rise above the challenges. I discovered the power of poetry when life got tough. For me, poetry was like a gentle breeze that calmed the storm.

I became a writer, and one of my most famous books is called "I Know Why the Caged Bird Sings." It's about my journey and the struggles I overcame. The title comes from a poem I wrote. It means a lot to me.

Because of my own struggles, I wanted to bring hope for others. When I wrote, I was lucky that my words flowed like a river. They often carried the stories of people who couldn't speak for themselves.

I met incredible leaders like Dr. Martin Luther King Jr., and together, we worked to make the world a more equal and fair place for everyone.

One of my favorite colors in my rainbow was courage. I stood tall and spoke up against injustice and I hoped to use my words to inspire change. I truly wanted to make the world a better place for everyone.

As the years went by, I collected more colors in my rainbow – love, wisdom, and kindness.

I met amazing friends who believed in me. Together, we made music with our words, turning the world into a symphony of acceptance and understanding.

My rainbow of words reached far and wide, touching the hearts of people all around the world. I realized that words have the power to heal, to unite, and to create a brighter tomorrow.

I received awards and honors, not because I wanted to be the best, but because I wanted to be a blessing to others. My heart overflowed with gratitude. I continued to write and share stories. I wanted every child to know that their voice matters, just like yours does.

One day, I looked back at my life and saw the magnificent rainbow I had created with my words.

So remember to paint your own rainbow with the colors of your dreams. Be kind, be brave, and never forget the magic that words can bring.

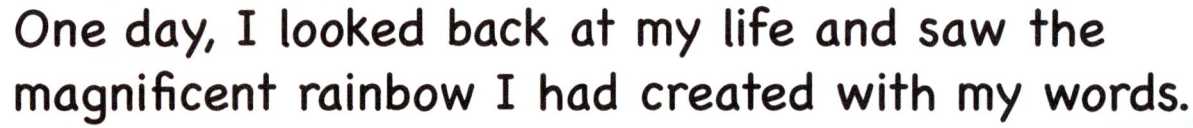

Timeline

1928 – Maya is born in St. Louis, Missouri

1957 – Maya records her first album, "Miss Calypso," which blends calypso, blues, and folk music.

1961 – Maya begins her involvement in the civil rights movement and works with Malcolm X.

1969 – Maya publishes her first autobiography, "I Know Why the Caged Bird Sings," which receives critical acclaim.

1970 – Maya collaborates with James Baldwin on the screenplay for the film "Georgia, Georgia," becoming one of the first African American women to have a screenplay produced.

1981 – Maya is appointed as a professor of American Studies at Wake Forest University in Winston-Salem, North Carolina.

2011 – Maya is awarded the Presidential Medal of Freedom by President Barack Obama.

I love hearing from my readers. Write to me at info@ninjalifehacks.tv or send mail to:

Mary Nhin
5 West 15th St.
Edmond, OK 73013

Visit minimovers.tv for lesson plans and more!

 @marynhin   @officialninjalifehacks
#minimoversandshakers

 Mary Nhin   Ninja Life Hacks

 Ninja Life Hacks

 @officialninjalifehacks

www.ingramcontent.com/pod-product-compliance
Lightning Source LLC
Chambersburg PA
CBHW041523070526
44585CB00002B/58